DO YOU KNOW

Hyenas?

Written by
**Alain M. Bergeron
Michel Quintin
Sampar**

Illustrations by
Sampar

Translated by
Solange Messier

Fitzhenry & Whiteside

First published as "Savais-Tu? Les Hyènes" by Editions Michel Quintin, Québec, Canada

Published in Canada by Fitzhenry & Whiteside, 195 Allstate Parkway, Markham, Ontario L3R 4T8

Published in the United States by Fitzhenry & Whiteside, 311 Washington Street, Brighton, Massachusetts 02135

www.fitzhenry.ca   godwit@fitzhenry.ca

10 9 8 7 6 5 4 3 2 1

Library and Archives Canada Cataloguing in Publication
Do You Know Hyenas?
ISBN 9781554553389 (pbk.)
Data available on file

Publisher Cataloging-in-Publication Data (U.S.)
Do You Know Hyenas?
ISBN 9781554553389 (pbk.)
Data available on file

Fitzhenry & Whiteside acknowledges with thanks the Canada Council for the Arts, and the Ontario Arts Council for their support of our publishing program. We acknowledge the financial support of the Government of Canada through the Canada Book Fund (CBF) for our publishing activities.

 Canada Council for the Arts Conseil des Arts du Canada

 ONTARIO ARTS COUNCIL CONSEIL DES ARTS DE L'ONTARIO
50 YEARS OF ONTARIO GOVERNMENT SUPPORT OF THE ARTS
50 ANS DE SOUTIEN DU GOUVERNEMENT DE L'ONTARIO AUX ARTS

Cover and text design by Daniel Choi
Cover image by Sampar
Printed in China by Sheck Wah Tong Printing Press Ltd.

Hyenas walk awkwardly because their back legs are shorter than their front legs.

There are three **species** of hyenas: the brown hyena, the striped hyena and the spotted hyena.

Its rough coat, shaggy mane, massive neck and hunched back give the hyena a less-than-elegant appearance.

The **carnivorous** hyena may be a **scavenger**, but it is also a skillful hunter.

Hyenas live in the extensive plains and savannas of Africa and Asia.

Hyenas are **nocturnal** and **crepuscular**.

During the day, hyenas rest in burrows, tall grass or rock crevices.

Hyenas have excellent hearing and an exceptional sense of smell. Their vision is also quite good.

Hyenas emit many sounds: yelps, grunts, growls, howls, screeches and cries.

21

The spotted hyena's most common cry is its energetic, crazy laugh.

Brown and striped hyenas live alone or in small families. They eat mostly small **prey**, fruit and **carrion**.

Spotted hyenas are rarely **solitary**. They usually live in clans that count from 10 to 30 hyenas, although there could be as many as 100 individuals in a group.

Members of the same clan recognize each other through their odours and their cries. Each individual hyena has a distinct, recognizable voice.

Any animal of another clan automatically triggers a strong reaction of fear and aggression.

Females dominate the clans. In fact, the adults dominate the young, and the females dominate the males.

It's often difficult to tell the difference between male and female hyenas. The female's external genitalia is often mistaken for that of the male's.

Hyenas play an important role in nature. By eating animal carcasses, they prevent the spread of disease.

The spotted hyena is the largest scavenger in the world.

The spotted hyena prefers to hunt zebras, wildebeest, gazelles and baby rhinoceros. However, it will also attack lions, buffalo, and aging or injured elephants.

Observers once watched 38 spotted hyenas devour an entire zebra carcass in 15 minutes.

Thanks to their powerful jaws, hyenas can even crush bone. They only leave behind the horns, hooves and fur of their victims.

Spotted hyenas also eat small animals, plants and **ungulate** dung.

Female hyenas give birth after a little more than three months of pregnancy. They give birth in burrows.

In the brown hyena species, the males also take care of the young.

Spotted hyena females raise their young together. They will even nurse each other's babies.

Hyenas from other clans pose a serious threat to spotted hyena cubs. Male hyenas are also a menace to the cubs.

To feed their young, hyenas bring home pieces of carcasses for the cubs to eat.

The hyena's only **predator** is the lion.

Spotted hyenas can live up to 20 years in the wild, while some have lived up to 40 years in captivity.

Glossary

Carnivorous a meat-eater

Carrion dead or decaying animal flesh

Crepuscular active during dawn and dusk

Nocturnal active at night

Predator a hunter that kills prey for food

Prey an animal hunted and killed by another for food

Scavenger an animal that eats dead or decaying matter

Solitary living alone

Species a classification for a group of creatures with common characteristics

Ungulate a large hoofed animal, such as a horse, rhinoceros or zebra

Index

Do You Know there are other titles?

Rats

Crows

Chameleons

Spiders

Porcupines

Crocodiles

Leeches

Toads

Komodo Dragons

Dinosaurs

Praying Mantises